W9-BHX-777

ALSO BY MARIE PONSOT

Springing

The Bird Catcher

The Green Dark

Admit Impediment

True Minds

Easy

Easy

Poems

MARIE PONSOT

ALFRED A. KNOPF   NEW YORK   2011

THIS IS A BORZOI BOOK
PUBLISHED BY ALFRED A. KNOPF

Published in the United States by Alfred A. Knopf,
a division of Random House, Inc., New York, and in Canada
by Random House of Canada, Limited, Toronto.

www.aaknopf.com

Knopf, Borzoi Books, and the colophon are registered
trademarks of Random House, Inc.

Library of Congress Cataloguing-in-Publication Data
Ponsot, Marie.
Easy : poems / by Marie Ponsot. — 1st ed.
p. cm.
ISBN 978-0-375-71187-9
1. Old age—Poetry.   2. Older people—Poetry.   I. Title.
PS3531.049E37 2009
811'.54—dc22   2009017488

Manufactured in the United States of America
Published October 20, 2009
First Paperback Edition, May 17, 2011

For Rosemary Deen,
who is incomparably magnanimous

Contents

I

I

ALHAMBRA IN NEW YORK

for Rosemary Deen

From the kitchen corner comes

the low electric hum

of the five-petaled fan.

A stir of air reaches us

sweetly, as if it were fresh;

it governs our breath.

Our talk over dinner

could not be better even

were we caressed (if

we were as we were)

by a skim of air lifting to us

moonstruck off the long pool

at Alhambra years ago, there

where we are, as we know.

IF LIVE, STONES HEAR

Where there are two

choose more than one.

In the longing of silence

             for sound

the longing of sound for

             silence

makes waves. Are the winds

of outer space

an utterance

or simply the rush of change

are rivers under our ground

audible to stones and to moles,

or is their wet self-storage

self-contained.

*

Between silence and sound

we are balancing darkness,

making light of it,

like the barren pear

that used to bloom

in front of Elaine's uplifting

Second Avenue,

like the acacia trees

perfuming the rue d'Alésia.

FOR DENIS AT TEN

He is a serious boy, a visitor.

He sees how an orchard of apple trees

opens this oriole morning

into a fossil-rock field where cattle

would stumble were there no rose-tangled

old walls of stone to hold them away.

Whistling, he is the serious city boy

who, given a country mission, strides

down the cow path, juggling a greening

to shy at recalcitrant rumps. He knows

he was sent. He goes on his own;

he takes into account

cows, chipmunk nutters, cowplats, sky!

& stones, holding each other into a wall,

and a black snake sunning, and, sky.

Birds slip brightness in among nettles and thistles.

It is early July. He was sent to the brook

beyond the pasture, for watercress.

He goes there, whistling.

       Nothing reminds him of something.

He sees what is there to see.

THIS BRIDGE, LIKE POETRY, IS VERTIGO

In a time of dearth bring forth number, weight, & measure.
—WILLIAM BLAKE

Describing the wind that drives it, cloud

rides between earth and space. Cloud

shields earth from sun-scorch. Cloud

bursts to cure earth's thirst.   Cloud

—airy, wet, photogenic—

is a bridge or go-between;

it does as it is done by.

It condenses. It evaporates.

It draws seas up, rains down.

I do love the drift of clouds.

Cloud-love is irresistible,

untypical, uninfinite.

Deep above the linear city this morning

the cloud's soft bulk is almost unmoving.

The winds it rides are thin;

it makes them visible.

As sun hits it or if sun

quits us it's blown away

or rains itself or snows itself away.

It is indefinite:

This dawns on me: no cloud is measurable.

Make mine cloud.

Make mind cloud.

The clarity of cloud is in its edgelessness,

its each instant of edge involving

in formal invention, always

at liberty, at it, incessantly altering.

A lucky watcher will catch it

as it makes big moves:

up the line of sight it lifts

until it conjugates or

      dissipates,

its unidentical being intact

though it admits flyers.

It lets in wings. It lets them go.

It lets them.

It embraces mountains & spires built

to be steadfast; as it goes on

it lets go of them.

         It is not willing.

         It is not unwilling.

Late at night when my outdoors is

indoors, I picture clouds again:

         Come to mind, cloud.

         Come to cloud, mind.

ALONGSIDE THE POND

At the edge of vision

just short of sight

pond air shimmers pearly

unbroken ungated. Bright

mist engages me

silent unmediated.

When I turn

and look into it

I want birds.

FIT AUDIENCE

for David Rothenberg

(*andante cantabile:*
G sharp is not G natural)

Mozart and his starling

both loved to whistle.

What a pair.

Maybe for just this once

in our history of Bird

we can forgive the uncaged cager.

Our god-besot Mozart

bought it caged it kept it,

a fabulous singer

priceless but with useless wings.

When it sang out

loud, careless, impetuous,

Mozart's shoulder blades ached

but he heard it sing.

HEAD TURKEY MUSES: A SOLILOQUY

"I spread my tail. You halt. I walk right by you, close up.

You let me. You'd better. You

have no choice. Back and forth

I edge you, by my walk.

Which is righteous. I've got

my game face on. I get

the angle of the beak just perfect—

up. It stops you short.

It pens you, helpless, to the spot.

I wait. A long beat. You freeze.

And I front you and you drop your head.

You admit my walk wins. I walk superior.

You? duck your little head, duck lower.

Good.   The ground feels warm.

My spurs get sharper every day.

I do not need to pen you anymore.

You know the score. You stay penned.

I am very busy. I am sentinel to

hens. I do them all. Not you. I do.

When crows scream Cover! I decide

to credit them. For your safety's sake

I fade my great red wattle down to pink.

When I take cover

everybody does.

You too. I keep an eye on your head (low)

and on your wattle (at all times, grey).

Geese overhead shout nonsense. I

gobble at them and they're gone. And you

are where I can see to you.

You stay. I let you stay."

ONE GRIMM BROTHER TO THE OTHER

"I've never lived inside the gingerbread house,

have you? I don't say I've never visited.

But never lived. I know I couldn't like to.

It's cramped and it stinks of being afraid.

Of what. Which am I. Who is she. Afraid

I'd hate to eat her & she'd make me sick.

Afraid she'd eat me last. First. Afraid

no sweet-tooth brat would fatten and be sweet

to roast & baste & eat. Afraid that once

I'd cooked them (& started a soup for stock—

full of oniongrass—I'd boil their bones to)

no more soft children would climb my candy fence

& nibble up the path to my cookie tree,

my door of chocolate (whose inside fear is

inside the fear inside),

afraid I'd catch my breath

& hear the swarm of mice squeak, 'Eat or die,'

and then I'd have to eat and I would die afraid."

PETER RABBIT'S MIDDLE SISTER

Mopsy, you were in your briar patch

birthplace the trustworthy sister, who ate

blackberries with cream & kept the floors swept.

You came back promptly when sent out to fetch

brown bread for supper, while your reprobate

brother adventured, broke things, got caught, leapt

free, lost his shirt, got scolded till you botched

your homework and cried for him till you slept.

Your grief was seeing him stand there wretched,

reproached for his deeds. Not he, you, wept,

your chest hot, your heart fast in the thorned clutch

of your hedge-hemmed root-safe bedtime-tale hutch.

We realist rabbits wrongly denigrate

the softhearted order of your careful state.

The green vine is moving.

The motion's too slow to be

visible but it is racing,

racing feeling for a way

across the wall of fence

it's scrawling on, inches added every day.

Forwarding, sunwarding, it claims

its place. Green states its claim. It writes

the lesson of the day: longing,

longing coming true while arcing

out and up according to the instruction

of desire. Sun-hungry its tip has tilted

toward sun-space. Already

it is speeding leaf-notes out of its root

all along the sprigless budless thread

still scribbling the deed of its location.

In two weeks or one or four

morning   glory.

THE WOLF AND THE LAMB
(La raison du plus fort est toujours la meilleure)
from JEAN DE LAFONTAINE, *Fables* I, 10

The strongest reasons are the reasons of the strong.

It's so—as we'll show before long.

A lamb was drinking quietly

close to the edge of a clear brook

which was on the path the wolf, when fasting, took.

The wolf eyed the lamb hungrily.

"Who's made you so brave you muddy my drink?" he cried,

cross as two sticks and fit to be tied.

"Such arrogance must be punished, don't you agree?"

"Sire," said the lamb, "may it please Your High Majesty

to be unenraged—and to note

that where I stand and wet my throat

is—as you, Sire, may see is true—

downstream from you,

downstream by twenty yards at least,

proof I can't possibly muddy your royal drink

from my low stance here at the brink."

"Wretch! You DO muddy it—and," said the cruel beast,

"what's worse, you told lots of lies about me last year."

"Not I! This year's my first; last year I wasn't here,"

said the lamb. "I'm still nursing my mother."

"Not you? Then it was your brother!"

"I have none."

"Then one of your kin.

You owe me, one way or the other,

you, your shepherd, your dogs, their kin—

I must take revenge. Your crimes are known."

Wolf dragged lamb under the trees

and cracked and ate him, blood and bone,

with no further formalities.

TO THE WINDS, FROM A WINNOWER OF WHEAT

translated from JOACHIM DU BELLAY, in honor of WILLIAM RYDING

Welcome, welcome, infant breeze,

lightly flying where you please.

Whisperer, why not whistle, too,

among the sun-struck grass.

Teach it to bend when you pass;

push less gently through.

I bring you these spring beauties,

lilies, violets, daisies,

and these notable roses,

these rosy briar clusters

whose split buds match the luster

this carnation discloses.

May your crescent breath soon reign

strong and clear across this plain.

Freshen this spot, where I stay

to work the wheat. I obey

the one true winnowing way

in the heat of the day.

LISTEN

clouds:

are they all

   soundless

(are you sure?)

A RUNE, INTERMINABLE

Low above the moss

a sprig of scarlet berries

soon eaten or blackened

tells time.

Go to a wedding

as to a funeral:

bury the loss.

Go to a funeral

as to a wedding:

marry the loss.

Go to a coming

as to a going:

unhurrying.

*

Time is winter-green.

Seeds keep time.

Time, so kept, carries us

across to no-time where

no time is lost.

ROUTE 80, SALT LAKE CITY TO RENO, BEAUTIFUL

for Ann Cosler Gallagher

The man at the dry gas station says he can recall,

maybe every nine or ten years, a hard rain then a rush

of carpeting flowers up sudden & small.

Not lately. And the dust-maker sun, alkaline

over a wound-scouring wind, sees to it

the flowers seed but leave no green sign.

This seascape of stone, its beige & grey stretched exposed

to ten hundred thousand winters, records

no events but those of rocks: WE EXPLODED—

announcing it in a seared continuous cry

to the vastness of empty unlistening

others call sky.

WALKING HOME FROM THE MUSEUM

The pleasure of walking, Brother Angel,

calls to mind your Paradise panel

of radiant saviors. They step the vertical

at ease in their deathlife, delectable.

You show among slow green leaves their bliss in place

in the vivid repose of each breathless face.

I lack leaves and their air-exchanging grace.

I lack gold leaf and your burin skill. Here I walk

east and west of death, toward their lute-led talk,

its pure sound spilt from song. In their words' embrace

strangers partner. Their redeeming speech spans

time and tune. Solo, they also move as a throng

conversing, hand lifted to open hand,

their speech sung as if not split from song.

II

WE OWN THE ALTERNATIVE

for Naomi Replansky, poet, and OWN, the Old Women's Network

"Mere failure to be young is not interesting,"

our host says. "Here we are free to be not young,

not bound to evaluate everything,

ready for Tuesday's flimsy shift to be flung

over Friday's shoulder, or for it to cling,

a comfort when cold winds make comfort disappear.

Old's our game. We've fought clear of innocence.

So we dress our acts up, or down. We veer

from chitchat to epics of our consequence.

Old lefty post-docs can read as they appear

words of doom or grace off the graffiti fence

of chance, and laugh out loud at what some fear.

We even grab a can and squirt our mark

now & then, in the now before then the dark."

POPULAR BINOCULARS

Opposites are mind's shorthand but don't exist

What soars from sight above, begins beneath.

Watch:

　　　up her beanstalk smart Jackie twists,

a climbing rose between her teeth,

to claim the virile task of Giant Slaughter

leaving her mother's milkmaid life below.

Exchanging roses with the Giant's Daughter,

she borrows Giant binoculars which show

the low world's working people, us, poor as piss,

all tired, some brave. She shouts, "My quest's below!

Come, Giant's Wife & Daughter, to Metropolis!"

They steal the Giant's stolen gold before they go.

They invest in Jackie's mother. They grow.

Two eyes yield one vision. Two sexes show

promise, like a prismatic synthesis.

SOLILOQUY AT THE BENEFIT EVENT

"The name of this performance is 'The New Wife'—

it's not about us old wives. It has to do

with 'young' meaning 'younger than.' Its set is rife

with screens for folded scenes that one miscue

might expose us to. What's her name, again?

(Wife I's our age.) She looks soft (like Wife II,

who blanked us like a hallucinogen).

Don't say, 'You know my son was at school with you.'

Poor thing. Best we just not mention children.

Wife I's better off—with debts, with custody—

without him. She'd want us to applaud

this girl, her looks, her style, his taste—though he

does look awkward, playing young, playing lord.

She's bored. He's scared. She's scared. He's bored."

CONTRACTED

Here comes her helpmeet

        at a trot.

He's a dealer in defeat;

        she is not.

Woe's what he's here for,

        not so, she,

proud of her bookstore

        at the mall.

No pride could look more

        like a fall.

DRIVE LIKE A LADY BLUES

No I won't stick to the back roads

when I go out to drive.

I'm not driving right-lane byways

just to keep that car alive.

No buzzwords no byways

no back roads no beehive. No.

I say I'm driving on the highway

at this time. I'm driving my way

on your highway, eat my dust,

Lord knows it ain't *my* tranny going bust.

TRAIN TO AVIGNON

Three international European young

homing toward Holland from Kasmir

complain, "This train stops everywhere."

They're headed for Arles to watch men stick bulls;

they think that might be interesting.

The fresh white head of my opposite number

turns from them; she inverts her smile, nods to me,

says the grand Avignon children she's going to see

handsomely repay her interest in them.

The Dutch drink Cola pop-top with their chips.

I halve a white-fleshed peach & eat summer raw.

I envy madame her unvarying knife cut;

salami & bread drop in classic rounds.

Prompt with Latin hosting courtesy,

once she learns I am a foreigner

we drink a wine, pale gold, drawn

from the grapes of her Burgundy acre.

She approves my raspberries, merely bought.

The young debate among themselves in Dutch.

Panicky, they don't know where they are. She

waits, then points (noting the asterisks

on her up-to-date non-crack train schedule)

to when they'll arrive. They sigh in relief.

She helps them endorse their rucksacks

& smiles them out into her customary world.

I've given them all my oranges.

We, extravagant, chat easily,

take our vagrant ease. We're off,

stopping & starting, off-season,

off-peak, on time, on our own.

LAST

Waste-pipe sweat, unchecked, has stained the floor

under the kitchen sink. For twenty years

it's eased my carelessness into a mean soft place,

its dirty secret dark, in a common place.

Today the pipe's fixed. Workmen rip up the floor

that's served and nagged me all these good/bad years.

They cut and set in new boards, to last for years.

House-kept no more, I waltz out of the place

clean-shod and leave no footprint on the floor,

displaced and unfloored. This year, nothing goes to waste.

SIMPLES

what do I want

well I want to

get better

LANGUAGE ACQUISITION

Burn, or speak your mind. For the oak to untruss

its passion it must explode as fire or leaves.

The delicious tongue we speak with speaks us.

A liquor of sweetness where its root cleaves

ripens fluent, as it runs for the desirous

reason, the touching sense. The infant says "I"

like earthquake and wavers as place takes voice.

Earth steadies smiling around her, in reply

to her self-finding pronoun, her focal choice.

We wait: while sun sucks earth juices up from wry

root-runs tangled under dark, while the girl

no longer vegetal, steps into view:

a moving speaker, an "I" the air whirls

toward the green exuberance of "You."

SEPTEMBER IN NEW YORK, PUBLIC & ELEMENTARY, 1927

As if speech could have sparks

leaping in it (the way they leap up

    when a new lover says, "Welcome home, love,"

    or a new softball captain says, "Let's go, gang!")

once upon a time she with her soft fast glance

collecting them said, "Good morning, class,"

and all her seated uplooking expectant

second-graders quickly said gladly,

    "Good morning, Miss McKnight,"

ready, hearts hammering,

her gang, her lovers, her class.

ON EASTER SATURDAY BELLS WHACKED THE AIR

Pet dogs help children. Spring after spring

two blaze-white Samoyeds sped me out

to my relief to run

into a new hush after the last noon clang

of church bells, rung ringing since dawn

to proclaim Easter Saturday—

        big bells, high up, and all of them

at once, let loose, a deafening glory

for my city of muted immigrants, plenty

of Catholics, bells just a few blocks apart,

Italy, Poland, Ireland, Germany, & Spain,

their metal tested, their cast full-voiced

non-liturgic, jubilee, wake up, hear this, look

out, resurrection, halleluia in yanked abandon

all morning—

        avenue traffic drowned out,

backyards & alleys humming in soundsurge,

and my breath a strong pulse

of everywhere hooray—no synchrony

no harmony no purity just hooray

just giant jubilee noise, dogs of course

not liking it, but for me utter

exultation rampant, though I loved my dogs

and took the run they gave me exalting

This is the day that the world hath made.

Rejoice and be glad therein.

WHAT SPEAKS OUT

Massive, a musical instrument

unplayed for four thousand years,

it's almost my height, caged

in museum glass,

ticketed:

It's a kind of lute, harplike, huge,

a lute made of solid silver (blackening).

At its foot is a slack tangle of strings,

and if strung taut if touched

it would thrum.

From its baseboard stares

the head of a boar made

by someone who had seen a boar.

Cornered, caved, tarnishing

regardless in the dark at the back

edge of a royal burial, it sucked

the dust of the three skulls

of three young women

whose heads it crushed

as it was planted there.

The human remains are listed as

still in Mesopotamia, informative

though not museum-quality, dated by scraps

of ribbon, bone, dress, beads, a plectrum.

Linens and skeletons

show they were tall girls, probably

two singers and a lutanist, untarnished,

breakable, intentional, faithful

servants and instruments of song.

ORPHANED OLD

I feel less lucky since my parents died.

Father first, then mother, have left me

out in a downpour

roofless in cold wind

no umbrella no hood no hat no warm

native place, nothing

between me and eyeless sky.

In the gritty prevailing wind

I think of times I've carelessly lost things:

      that white-gold ring when I was eight,

      a classmate named Mercedes Williams,

      my passport in Gibraltar,

      my maiden name.

WHY VOW

Hopkins (some say, daft) holds

that his self is unlost, a fact,

unchanged by its unfolding

as it stands for his each act.

Self (daft or not) lives out its vow:

his now is a perpetual now.

Obedient: he said he would.

He did as he said. He did

as he was told. He could

good as gold, hold good.

MAGNANIMOUS, MAGNIFICENT

Dump the jump-cuts, gentlemen. Steady on.

Try a kick-start to warm your kept cool and

your chic smiles lightly perverti. For once,

laugh at each other's jokes, don't top them,

simmer down, take the next step.

Propose lunch, or even dinner with your wives

(waiting all this competitive time for

you to look lovable again, to come with them to table).

Take notice, praise their shaky grace. Say Please.

Lay your cards on the linen faceup

causing a music to start. Listen—

it's music for dancing, so you dance.

Say you like it. Admit you've had some good luck.

Thank your friends for arriving on time. To the others,

the ones you dream of as enemies,

smile and say Thank you, and then try to mean it.

As the music stops you'll miss its lilt.

Keep dancing, keep listening. Speak up.

Ask for more music, more. In case you don't know,

what you want is magnificent, yours for the asking,

the rhythm of magnanimous exchange.

TV, EVENING NEWS
—seen on CNN, autumn 2005, Afghanistan

It's a screenful of chaos but

the cameraman's getting good framing shots

from behind one woman's back.

The audio's poor. The shouts are slices of noise.

I don't know the languages.

No hot hit heroes are there.

No wicked people are there.

Achilles is not there, or Joshua either.

Rachel is not there, nor Sojourner Truth.

Iwo Jima flag boys? not there.

Twin Towers first defenders? not there.

My children are thank God not there

any more or less than you and I are not there.

I safe screen-watch. A youth

young in his uniform

signals his guard squad

twice: OK go, to the tanks

and the cameramen: OK go.

The tank takes the house wall.

The house genuflects. The tank proceeds.

The house kneels. The roof dives.

The woman howls. Dust rises.

They cut to the next shot.

The young men and the woman

breathe the dust of the house

which now is its prayer.

A dust cloud rises, at one

with the prayer of all the kneeling houses

asking to be answered

and answerable anywhere.

III

THANK GERARD

Cascade: rain torrential rain

waterfalls down our stone facade.

Our fields lately fire-parched

now glossy cross the flat rise

you ploughed earlier. The whole

length of one sillion-streak gleams

Gerard

cut-stroke the sillion the gash

we have in mind is your mind

                lifting muck-life

turned sunstruck to each side

silvershot at low sunset after the rain

every drop cataract

             *

is not this the rain

we have longed for, you and I

God   to you

hold him close-folded

above his sillion

Loft him Halo him

Prize him high, pen in hand

his two uprooted feet

flailing awkward rain-streaked

below his healing blooded knees.

THE GOOD

The plot is simple: a traveling man

is mugged on a lonely street, robbed, beaten,

and left to bleed. The few who hear his groans

won't stop. They don't want to get sucked in.

Then he hears someone: a Samaritan

salesman from the ghetto. He groans again

& it works. He's saved.

                    As I gnaw this old bone

I sink to the marrow: my late father, in sudden

fresh recall. He said righteousness is shown

less by the short halt to help a stranger than

by evoking others' genius, then going on

to do the work that he knew was his own.

Mercy praises Justice: the Samaritan

acts to do exactly all he can.

AGAINST FIERCE SECRETS

Only to themselves are the passionate

hot. To the objects of their passion they

are cold. What Yeats knew. They eradicate

what they notice, as the thumb hard-crams the clay

impressionable under it, to lie flat,

apt to the shape their cold-steel scribes may

cut or spurn it to. Yet they know passion

must drown to ripen sweet & give fair play

to the whole life hot passion speeds us from.

As passion's object, dig with your ampersand:

be cold & hot. The receptive earth will come

to transform the root-end that your planting hand

cut & abandoned, to new chrysanthemum.

Heartfelt thought, drop your guard, keep clear, be slow;

double your careful opposites & grow.

ON LINE

Over the rootspread of woods, words, turf

we walk, talking, through the blue hour.

In each of us, the rootspreads outline

a universe at its origin.

We reach the lakeshore.

We row out into the dark.

We fish all night, no nets. Sometimes

we weight or bait each other's hooks,

testing what our lines can catch.

May the lakelife prosper.

May the hooks we remove

    do minimal damage.

May the lines hold good.

COMETING

I like to drink my language in

straight up, no ice no twist no spin

—no fruity phrases, just unspun

words trued right toward a nice

idea, for chaser. True's a risk.

Take it I say. Do true for fun.

We say water is taught by thirst

      earth by ocean diving

      birds by the lift of the heart

      oh that lift

      —curative, isn't it—

      a surge a sursum   as

      words become us

      we come alive lightly

      saying Oh

         *

at the wordstream of sentences

transparent in their consequence

cometing before our eyes

trailing crystalline

across our other sky

and we drink from it

    for the jolt of language

    for its lucid hit

    of bliss, the surprise.

FRANCE, AS FIRST DAUGHTER OF ROME

The tiny hillchurch that would, if full, hold

some thirty folk, is locked and disaffected

from the cult, save for one day a year when

on the feast of its saint a priest drives in

to suit up & celebrate the Mass,

bloodless after two thousand bloody years.

Grumbling, pairs of villagers shift gears

to reach church in first gear, though that wastes gas.

At home, on low heat, dinner simmers;

they've put their old-time pre-TV faces on,

left pills & condoms shelved by the bedstead.

They de-car here where the rite will unfold

its gestures meant to localize infinity

as one old man knows.

                One may be plenty.

ART: OLD AS NEW

When wishes composed me

but couldn't come true,

when dreams spoke girl-Latin

(well, I was new)

I met works of genius

expectant and thirsty.

I still do. So do you.

Still unimproved, thirsty, expectant,

we house them remembered

inside, where armed and endangered,

we live by the replay that gratifies

the thirst it rectifies.

WHAT *IS* IS

True high is true deep.

True pebble's true stone.

She is not a true sheep.

She is a true clone.

RECOVERY

I recover my history

and my chairs

with brilliant fabrics,

putting on airs

of luminous usefulness

and captivating pattern.

Of course, my dears,

they can't be sat in.

FOR ROBERT RAUSCHENBERG

The door I bought is a door with three lights.

A door with three lights is nonetheless

solid, somewhat, penetrated and yet

sometimes somewhat impassable.

Open or shut it's part opaque,

part holey, like me not definite,

so I'll hang this door gladly.

I admit the doors of perception are

cleansed only momently as

they open in on the ward of light.

    invitational: do come, light.

        shadow, do come, do.

    institutional: here's the clean-up squad;

        here's the vinegary window-washer;

        here's the hopeful tidier-upper;

    please indicate where they should begin.

*

Shouldering aside the praising critic,

the painter explains, "Much to see

but not much showing."

BLISS AND GRIEF

No one

is here

right now.

SKEPTIC
for Helen DeMott, painter of waves

"I watch the heaving moving

of great waters. I read their surfaces.

Motion patterns them. Water

expresses the sea floor it is moved by.

Language thinks us. Myth or mouth

we migrants are its mystery.

It's our tension floats those halcyons

we want to say are safe

riding the wave-swell,

on the surface of some sea."

"Try telling that to the lookout sailor

his ship headed into the storm

headed for floundering.

Oh, I believe in storms all right,

and in ships that skim or sink,

and in some birds, some sailors.

But a scupper of a place of peace,

a nest-sized cupping and two

lovebirds calm in it?

No matter how much we want such peace,

no matter who believes in it (mouth or myth)

the tale of peace in a love nest in stormcalm

would only bewilder

us crow's nest sailors looking ahead

about to drown."

TRANSPORT

The rose, for all its behavior,

is smaller than the lifelove it stands for,

only briefly brightening,

and even its odor

only a metaphor.

Or so we suppose

just as we suppose the savior

we employ or see next door

is only some hired man

gardening.

IMAGINING STARRY

The place of language is the place between me

and the world of presences I have lost

—complex country, not flat. Its elements free-

float, coherent for luck to come across;

its lines curve as in a mental orrery

implicit with stars in active orbit,

only their slowness or swiftness lost to sense.

The will dissolves here. It becomes the infinite

air of imagination that stirs immense

among losses and leaves me less desolate.

Breathing it I spot a sentence or a name,

a rescuer, charted for recovery,

to speak against the daily sinking flame

& the shrinking waters of the mortal sea.

MIGRANT AMONG US

The otherworld is this world heeded

so well it swims in close to us,

its echo and shadow a swivel

of unintended attention.

Take notice: the otherworld

is lustrous, like sealight or

twilight, ambiguous because

it's more than one thing at a time:

      like the summer forward-thrust

      of the rackety local rivulet

      hurrying its loud brown

      water to its little fall,

      or like those of us who both

               *

track the stars and also

fly earthward at night

like migrant bird flocks—

as if the dark were flared,

as if we can see in the dark,

and we almost can.

REACHING

My plane takes off on time, and so do I.

The journey it charts charts me as I fly;

sight flashes into thought. I stare in at it

though (mapped as thought-through) the map lines lie

loopy. Thought goes too far, stretching to explain

my self, its selves, and how they move to unify.

They rush to catch the bright becoming point

thought casts before them like a light to work by.

The plane's nose always gets there first. I sit

belated, in the cabin section of the plane.

I'm my observer. I maneuver to join

my old self to its avant-garde, my eyes.

Sight likes travel which likes fresh surprises.

Self likes surprise that undoes old disguises.

TESTING GARDENING

In the garden I watch myself take care

as if I were the garden. I even learn

from experience! Slowly (fair is fair),

I may grow less stupid and learn to turn

error to advantage—though mistakes take

years of uprooting seedlings sprung from seed

dropped a decade ago in error's long wake.

I was right to want you, to sweat, weed,

balance acid soil, shield you from sunscald

early, then prune to make sure the sun you need

found you. For these few spring weeks you're a sprawl

of flowers, you green the summer toward its rest

in fruited autumn. Yet it's winter that's best,

yes, to imagine joy, next. The winter test.

PHYSICAL TRAINING

Spelled out in the body, history is slow.

My label reads: cryptic amateur, adept

at dailiness. Crow's-feet, muscles, scars have kept

the record of its waves, high tide and low.

I begin to learn to read its common sense:

    Sun-squint breakfast foreplay. Triumphs. Defeats.

    Lobster bisque. The wet-wash weight of linen sheets.

    Freeborn words. The broken kitchen. The open air

    of public walkways . . .

                I read the honey-striped

turn of body caught off guard, its full text ripe.

Its random list or life is in good repair.

Grateful, grateful, my hand slow to turn the page

turns it, labeled grateful, already engaged.

DANCING DAY I

At the horizon's lit fog rim

earth keeps in touch with sky.

I call this the end of the beginning.

In its mist, frayed ghosts of selves drowse;

I call them my lost selves.

Lately they drift close, unaging,

watching me age. Now & then, one or some

flare up, known shapes in known clothes.

Each of them is not not me, and wears

the clothes I walked in, joked, worked hurt in,

as I played my sweet pipsqueak part

paradiddle on the hi-hat.

I still know all those moves.

*

I begin to remember; I remember them,

some from when my father was alive.

A deep breath taken. Restorative.

They hum soft part-songs, hard to hear.

And now they're singing. They've come to stay!

It's turning into a party.

I put out bread, plates, glasses, grapes,

apples, napkins, pretzels, Bleu des Causses.

They whistle old signals. In our one name

we agree to our selving. I do agree.

                        I'll propose a toast,

why not. Time to let go. Get going.

Out of the cellar I take, ripe,

the rest of the case of Clos de Vougeot.

DANCING DAY II

Once, one made many.

Now, many make one.

The rest is requiem.

We're running out of time, so

we're hurrying home to

practice to

gether for the general dance.

We're past get-ready, almost at get-set.

Here we come many to

dance as one.

Plenty more lost selves keep arriving, some

we weren't waiting for. We stretch and

lace up practice shoes. We mind our manners—

no staring, just snatching a look

      —strict and summative—

at each other's feet & gait & port.

*

Every one we ever were shows up

with world-flung poor triumphs

flat in the backpacks we set down to greet

each other. Glad tired gaudy

we are more than we thought

& as ready as we'll ever be.

We've all learned the moves, separately,

from the absolute dancer

    the foregone deep breather

the original choreographer.

Imitation's limitation—but who cares.

We'll be at our best on dancing day.

        On dancing day

we'll belt out tunes we'll step to

together

till it's time for us to say

there's nothing more to say

    nothing to pay   no way

    pay no mind   pay no heed

    pay as we go.

Many is one; we're out of here,

exeunt omnes

    exit   oh and save

    this last dance for me

on the darkening ground

looking up into

the last hour of left light

in the star-stuck east,

its vanishing flective, bent

breathlessly.

Acknowledgments

"Train to Avignon" appeared in *Ploughshares*.

"Thank Gerard" appeared in *American Poet*.

"September in New York" appeared in *New York's Book Country 25th Anniversary Collection*.

"Cometing" appeared in *The New York Times* (Op-Ed).

"Against Fierce Secrets," "Language Acquisition," "Imagining Starry," "Late Spring," and "On Easter Saturday" appeared in *Commonweal*.

"Alhambra in New York" appeared in *The Journal*.

A NOTE ABOUT THE AUTHOR

Marie Ponsot's most recent books include *The Bird Catcher*, winner of the National Book Critics Circle Award for poetry in 1998, and *Springing: New and Selected Poems*. Professor emerita of English at Queens College, CUNY, she now teaches at the Unterberg Poetry Center of the 92nd Street Y and at the New School University. Her awards include the Phi Beta Kappa Medal, the Shaughnessy Prize of the Modern Language Association, and the Poetry Society of America's Frost Medal for lifetime achievement. Ponsot, a recently elected Chancellor of the Academy of American Poets, lives in New York City.

A NOTE ON THE TYPE

This book was set in Adobe Garamond. Designed for the Adobe Corporation by Robert Slimbach, the fonts are based on types first cut by Claude Garamond (c. 1480–1561). Garamond was a pupil of Geoffroy Tory and is believed to have followed the Venetian models, although he introduced a number of important differences, and it is to him that we owe the letter we now know as "old style." He gave to his letters a certain elegance and feeling of movement that won their creator an immediate reputation and the patronage of Francis I of France.

Composed by Creative Graphics,
Allentown, Pennsylvania

Printed and bound by Thomson-Shore, Inc.,
Dexter, Michigan

Designed by Soonyoung Kwon